VOLCANO

Kitchen Experiment

By Meg Gaertner

Published by The Child's World®
1980 Lookout Drive • Mankato, MN 56003-1705
800-599-READ • www.childsworld.com

Photographs ©: Rick Orndorf, cover, 1, 14, 16, 17, 18, 19, 20,
21; Tatsiana Kuryanovich/Shutterstock Images, 5; Shutterstock
Images, 6; iStockphoto, 7, 9, 12; Sharon Dominick/
iStockphoto, 10; Steve Debenport/iStockphoto, 13

ISBN 9781503825345
LCCN 2017959655

Printed in the United States of America
PA02378

Table of Contents

CHAPTER 1

Volcanoes

A volcano is a mountain with a hole in its middle. The hole goes deep into the ground. It is very hot there. The rock melts. This melted rock is called magma. It is less heavy than the rock around it. The magma rises through the hole in the volcano.

Sometimes the hot magma moves very quickly. It **erupts**. Magma spills out of the hole. It becomes **lava**. It runs down the mountain.

Some volcanoes do not erupt anymore. Others are still active.

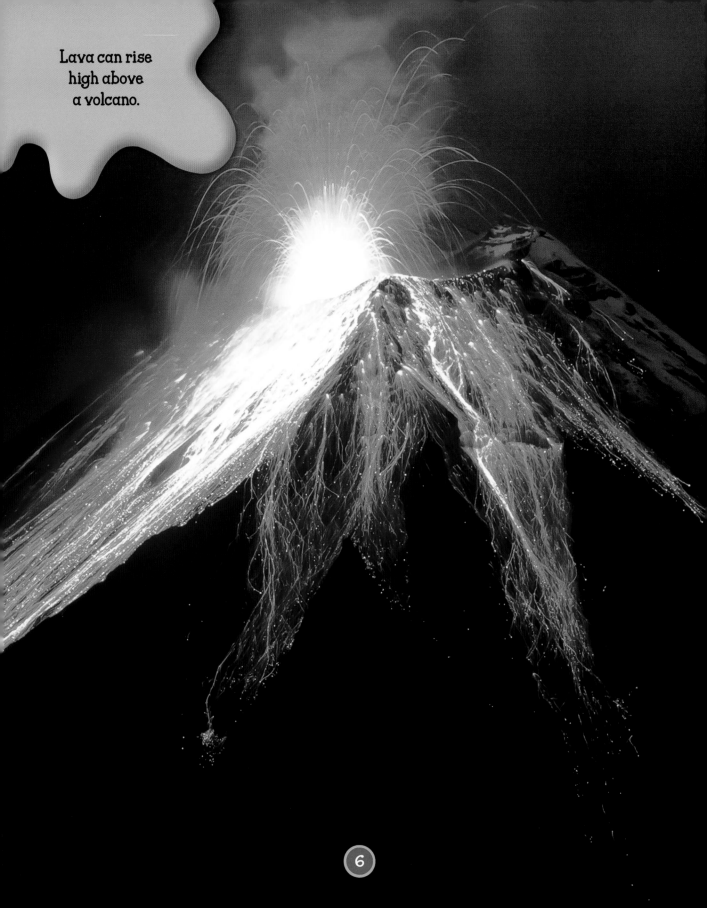

Lava can rise
high above
a volcano.

Mixing two liquids together will sometimes make a reaction.

The lava cools down. It becomes rock. This rock makes the volcano bigger.

You can make a volcano erupt in your kitchen! It is not dangerous. We will make a volcano using a **reaction**.

CHAPTER 2

Chemical Reactions

Everything is made of **atoms**. They are very tiny. We can't see them without special machines. An **element** is made of one type of atom. **Oxygen** is an element. We write it like this: O. Oxygen is in the air we breathe. **Hydrogen** is also an element. We write it like this: H. Hydrogen is the lightest gas.

A **molecule** is made of different types of atoms. Water is a molecule. It is made of two hydrogen atoms and one oxygen atom.

We can't see atoms. But we can make models to look at their shapes.

A glass of water is filled with many H_2O molecules.

We can write water like this: H_2O. One water molecule can split into two parts. One hydrogen atom stays by itself. We write that like this: H+.

The other atoms go together. We write that like this: OH-.

A **chemical** is made of a specific set of atoms. Water is a chemical. It is always H_2O. Two chemicals come together in a reaction. They change to become something new.

A reaction happens when an **acid** mixes with a **base**. An acid has a lot of hydrogen atoms (H+). Milk and fruit juices are acids. A base has a lot of hydrogen and oxygen atoms (OH-). Soap is a base.

TIP
A reaction makes your bike rust after it rains. Bikes have bits of iron in them. Iron is shiny and smooth. It breaks down when it mixes with water. It becomes bumpy and brown with rust.

An acid does not always mean something is dangerous. Milk is an acid. It is safe to drink.

We will make a reaction using vinegar (an acid) and baking soda (a base). When they mix, they change into a gas. This will make our kitchen volcano erupt.

Sometimes reactions with acids and bases can be messy!

CHAPTER 3

THE EXPERIMENT
Let's Make a Volcano!

MATERIALS LIST

tape
5 pieces of construction paper
baking dish or pan
1 empty plastic 12-ounce (355 mL) bottle
scissors
2 tablespoons (28 g) baking soda
funnel
food coloring
10 ounces (296 mL) warm water
straw
6 drops liquid dish soap
2 ounces (59 mL) vinegar

TIME TO FINISH: 15-30 minutes

15

30

1. Tape one piece of construction paper to the inside of the baking dish.

2. Wrap one piece of construction paper around the plastic bottle. Tape the paper together. Make sure that the paper is not taller than the bottle.

3. Tape the bottom of the bottle to the middle of the baking dish.

4. Cut three pieces of construction paper into long strips. Tape one end of a strip to the top of the paper around the bottle. Tape the other end to the baking dish.

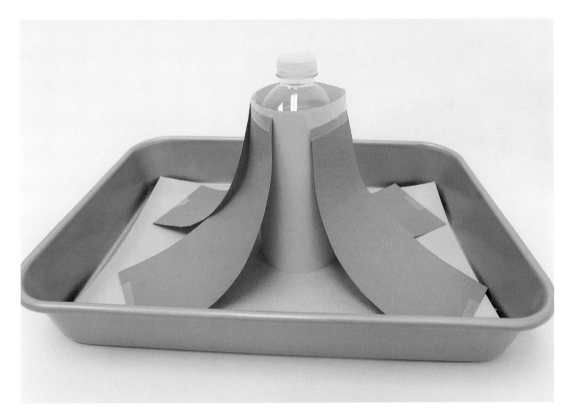

5. Keep taping more pieces of paper. Make sure that the paper is not covering the hole in the bottle.

6. Add baking soda to the bottle with the funnel.

7. Add a few drops of food coloring.

8. Fill the bottle most of the way with warm water. Remove the funnel. Mix everything in the bottle using the straw.

9. Add 6 drops of dish soap to the bottle. Mix slowly with the straw.

10. Add vinegar to the bottle. Quickly move your hand. Watch it erupt!

TIP

You can keep the reaction going by adding more vinegar and baking soda. The more vinegar and baking soda you use, the bigger the reaction.

Glossary

acid (ASS-id) An acid gives off many hydrogen atoms. Fruit juice is an acid.

atoms (AT-uhms) Atoms make up everything we see. Atoms come together to make elements.

base (BAYSS) A base gives off a lot of hydrogen and oxygen atoms. A base reacts with an acid in a chemical reaction.

chemical (KEM-uh-kuhl) A chemical is made of a special set of atoms. Water is a chemical.

element (EH-luh-mint) An element is something made from one type of atom. Oxygen is an element.

erupts (i-RUHPTS) A volcano erupts when magma comes out very quickly. The magma that erupts becomes lava.

hydrogen (HYE-druh-juhn) Hydrogen is a gas. There are two hydrogen atoms in every water molecule.

lava (LAH-vuh) Lava is magma that comes out of a volcano. Lava flows down the side of the volcano.

molecule (MOL-uh-kyool) A molecule is a group of different types of atoms. Water is a molecule.

oxygen (OK-suh-juhn) Oxygen is a gas. There is one oxygen atom in every molecule of water.

reaction (ree-ACK-shuhn) A reaction happens when two chemicals are mixed together. Rust is a reaction.

To Learn More

In the Library

Galat, Joan Marie. *Erupt! 100 Fun Facts about Volcanoes.*
Washington, DC: National Geographic Children's Books, 2017.

Navarro, Paula, and Ángels Jiménez. *Incredible Experiments
with Chemical Reactions and Mixtures.* Hauppage, NY: Barron's
Educational Series, 2014.

Rusch, Elizabeth. *Will It Blow? Become a Volcano Detective at
Mount St. Helens.* Seattle, WA: Little Bigfoot, 2017.

On the Web

Visit our Web site for links about volcanoes:
childsworld.com/links

Note to Parents, Teachers, and Librarians: We routinely verify our Web links to make
sure they are safe and active sites. So encourage your readers to check them out!

Index

About the Author

Meg Gaertner is a children's book author and editor who lives in Minnesota. When not writing, she enjoys dancing and spending time outdoors.